THE ILLUSTRATED DISCOVERY JOURNAL

THE ILLUSTRATED DISCOVERY JOURNAL

*Creating a Visual Autobiography
of Your Authentic Self*

S A R A H   B A N   B R E A T H N A C H

WARNER BOOKS

A TIME WARNER COMPANY

Warner Books, Inc., 1271 Avenue of the Americas, New York, NY 10020
Visit our Web site at www.warnerbooks.com

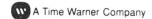 A Time Warner Company

Printed in the United States of America
First Printing: October 1999
10 9 8 7 6 5 4 3 2 1

ISBN: 0-446-52144-2
LC: 99-63730

Design by Kathleen Herlihy-Paoli, Inkstone Design

CONTENTS

INTRODUCTION

But if you have nothing at all to create,
then perhaps you create yourself.

—CARL JUNG

WELCOME. THIS IS A BOOK ABOUT YOU, FOR YOU, by you—a visual autobiography of your glorious, gutsy, Authentic Self. "Since you are like no other being ever created since the beginning of Time, you are incomparable," the marvelous author Brenda Ueland wrote in 1938. Please hold this thought as we begin a guided pilgrimage together on these pages. We're headed to the sacred site of your soul, one of the last unlooted sources of the miraculous left in this world.

Virginia Woolf believed that very few women write truthful memoirs, and I know why. Memory—the vain old biddy—cannot resist penciling in a few slight cosmetic revisions in the margins of our past, revisionist recollections intended to mirror back to the world the very best versions we can conjure up of our very false selves—

masquerades meant to disguise our secret self-loathing and desperate desire to be love by anyone at any cost.

It takes courage to be authentic in a culture content with only conformity However, embracing your authenticity is the only way you learn to become content with *your* life. Becoming authentic also takes knowledge. *Self-knowledge.* "You can live a life time and, at the end of it, know more about other people than you know about your self," Beryl Markham wrote in *West with the Night.*

Not if you keep an Illustrated Discovery Journal.

How happy are you right now? Do you even know? In my twenties I though fame would make me happy. In my thirties, I knew the secret to happiness was mar riage and a baby. On my fortieth birthday, with my little girl and husband blowing ou the candles with me, I became convinced that a comma in my checking account bal ance was the answer to my restless search. But it was only after I wrote a book on how to be happy despite not having any or all of the above (which became a best-seller because there were a lot of women just like me) that I came to the awareness—thank God—that happiness is dependent on one thing: self-worth. But before you can hold yourself in esteem, you have to know what you love and how magnificent you truly are.

More often than not, we discover who we are and what we love through reve- lations found in the small, the simple, and the common. In tiny choices; in what seem like infinitesimal changes. In the unconsidered. The overlooked. The discarded. The reclaimed. In moments I call everyday epiphanies. When those "ah-*ha*" transmissions allow the static of the world suddenly to clear and the soul's Morse code—the dots and dashes of our daily round, so often dismissed as meaningless—not only connects but resonates on a deep level.

Many of my everyday epiphanies have occurred when I have been pleasantly immersed in my Illustrated Discovery Journal.

You've heard the expression "One picture's worth a thousand words"? Well, it's true. In fact, I've discovered, to my astonishment, as will you, that random pictures— images culled from periodicals, cut out of catalogs, photographs, or postcards—when reverently and reflectively assembled by your own hands into a collage can reveal just about anything you might ever want to know about yourself, from the prosaic to the profound. Your passions. Your preferences. The perfect haircut. What tickles you. What ticks you off. What makes you happy.

"An image is a bridge between evoked emotion and conscious knowledge," the Mexican poet Gloria Anzaldùa tells us. "Images are more direct, more immediate than words, and closer to the unconscious." Maybe this sounds so suspiciously easy you're sure there's bound to be a catch, such as requiring an artistic talent you're convinced you don't possess. (You do—you just don't know it yet. Wait!) But I swear to you that the woman you truly are is patiently waiting to be revealed on the pages of this Illustrated Discovery Journal, and I'm going to show you how to coax her out of hiding after decades of denial.

I'll even make you two promises.

The first is that you cannot do the Illustrated Discovery Journal incorrectly. Unlike any other area of your existence, it's impossible to make a mistake. (I'm the one who made this up—I should know.) My second promise is that while creating your Illustrated Discovery Journal, you'll experience goose-bump shivers of recognition, heartfelt moments of reconnection, and an amazing amount of fun. Think seven years old and a brand-new set of paper dolls. You've probably forgotten you could have this much fun indulging in a purely healthy addiction—but you will.

SNIPPETS OF SELF

One cannot divine nor forecast the conditions that will make happiness," Willa Cather reminds us. "One only stumbles upon them by chance, in a lucky hour." I literally stumbled upon the magical art of collage when I was in my twenties. During that time I was going through a confusing period, trying to define myself as an artist. Although I had studied theater and felt confident as an actress, I hesitated to call myself an artist because I couldn't throw a pot or draw a face and end up with a vase or visage that was recognizable. And yet the visual always spoke to my soul in intimate, intriguing, and imaginative ways. Then one day I read about Pablo Picasso's belief that "the artist is a receptacle for emotions that come from all over the place; from the sky, from the earth, from a scrap of paper, from a passing shape, from a spider's web." My heart felt as if Spirit had opened a door in my soul that I'd latched from the inside!

Almost instantly I began to revise my take on what constituted "art." I started to experiment with fast-drying acrylic paint, filling the canvases with impressionistic montages of color and form: the glint of light in the mirror above my dresser, pink tulips in a vase, one of my favorite hats. One afternoon I was holding two buttons I had pulled off of a vintage jacket, trying to reproduce their lovely blue color on my painter's palette. In a careless moment, I lost my grip on the buttons and they fell onto the half-finished canvas. Surprised, I looked at the buttons, stuck at an angle into the paint, as if I'd never seen

them before. Isn't this interesting? I thought, and so I left them there. The next day I added
a Victorian photograph of a woman; the next a funny headline from the newspaper; the
next, a piece of tulle veiling. Each day another wild object found its way to the canvas. By
the end of the week I had a visual hodgepodge that completely fascinated me and intrigued
others. One admirer, a hairstylist, even bought the collage for his shop! I suspected I was
onto something more than augmenting the rent with my art, and I was right.

THE MYSTICAL CHAIN
OF CHANCE

Dropping those buttons set in motion a mystical chain of chance. I began to play
more and more with collage, reserving all judgment as I experimented. By allowing
myself to do anything on the canvas (and do it badly), I felt emotionally unencumbered.
For the first time in my life, I was set free from the insidious but self-imposed cycle of
expectation and disappointment. Ironically, this happened because I didn't label myself
an artist. I just called it playing. Eventually I began to leave the paint completely out of
my creations; using only a pair of scissors, glue, and some magazine clippings, I discovered I could create art that revealed my truth on paper. This art was smaller in scale,
but much more personal, specific, and telling. Collage became an insight tool that I used
to excavate my own aesthetic, emotional, and intellectual preferences. With tiny snip-
pets and suspended disbelief, I began to become acquainted with a fascinating woman
of depth and mystery: my Authentic Self.

   I felt serene and contented when I was working on my collages, so whenever I
became really stressed out, I began to turn to collage as a remedy to get my mind off my
worries. Gradually, through many different kinds of frustrating situations, from brood-
ing over love gone awry to making career decisions, from money problems to decorating dilemmas, I discovered I could use collage to cut through my own confusion and
indecisiveness. As I made a collage using what I thought were casually selected images,
I would ask myself the anxiety-producing question, then meditate upon it slowly as I
glued the images down on paper. Then I would ceremoniously put it aside in a special
folder. Three or four days later, when I looked at the collage again, I usually broke through
my own bafflement, and a solution, or, at the very least, a new way of thinking about my
situation, would emerge. As the photographer Carolyn Kenmore points out, in life as

well as art, "It is the unexpected, hit-or-miss, instant impulse, these strange accidents, this surrealistic serendipity" out of which great things are born.

A PRIVATE ORACLE

In his book *The Art and Craft of Collage*, Simon Larbalestier explains the French origins of the words *collage, montage,* and *assemblage.* "Collage comes from *coller* (to stick), while montage derives from *monter* (to mount) and assemblage from *assembler* (to bring together)." By definition collages are artistic compositions made up of various materials such as paper, fabric, and wood, and their history is a long one. A thousand years ago Japanese poets and calligraphers created collage poems depicting landscape scenes dotted with cut-out shapes of trees and birds. In the seventeenth and eighteenth centuries, European religious collages featuring saints were popular. During the Russian Revolution in 1917, collages were used to express political propaganda, and in the 1970s Andy Warhol turned the collage into the height of pop art.

In these instances, collage was used as a communication tool to bring a message or idea to the public in a new and unusual way, through subjective interpretation. I believe you'll find collage to be an incredibly powerful, imaginative, and enjoyable way to bring new messages to yourself. Think of each collage you create in this book as a detailed dispatch from your subconscious mind to your awakened self. Want to know your future? Forget tarot cards or the Ouija board. Within these pages your own private oracle is waiting to be consulted.

DAYSCAPES

Our dreams—our Technicolor nightscapes—are ethereal collages. Dream canvases are filled with the illogical juxtaposition of snatches of conversations, people, and situations, such as a woman reciting the Declaration of Independence as she skis while serving tea to her church choir. Most of the time there seems to be no rhyme or reason to these dreams, but if we're willing to reflect on them, they make perfect sense. Actually, dreams are our spiritual Illustrated Discovery Journal. The difference is that in dreams our images come to us unsolicited and often out of anxiety; in our Discovery

Journal we actively choose the images that console, comfort, intrigue, and delight. We induce pleasurable reveries by creating personalized daydreams on paper.

MONOGRAMMED MUSINGS

Now it's time to get started.* You need these tools: a stack of magazines and mail-order catalogs from which you'll cut images of anything that pleases you—from clothing, home furnishings, and travel adventures to children's faces, gorgeous landscapes, and wacky ads; a pair of small sharp scissors; glue sticks; stickers; rubber stamps; and colored pencils (the watercolor ones are wonderful because, after you draw, you can go over your work with water on a paintbrush and—voilà!—you're a painter).

Don't forget to peruse foreign publications for some of your images. Experiment with British women's magazines (which you can often find at large newsstands) because they are so completely different in layout and design from our homegrown ones. Their fresh visuals and witty headlines always get my creative juices flowing.

Now, how often should you get out your Illustrated Discovery Journal? Reveling in this pastime twice a week will produce remarkable results. One night you cut, the next night you paste. I suggest you do this in the evening because, after the house is quiet, you're better able to unwind. Besides, this pastime is more effective if you're in a drowsy, relaxed, and receptive state as you glean authentic visual clues. Create a ritual around your monogrammed musing. I always light a beautiful scented candle, enjoy a glass of wine or a soothing cup of ginger tea, and listen to some favorite instrumental music (no lyrics to distract) as I play in my Discovery Journal. A wonderful way to use music as a creative thread when you work on projects that are started and stopped over a period of time (such as writing, sculpting, pottery, painting, or handicrafts) is to listen to the same music each time you work; your brain will immediately switch tracks and refocus your attention to where you left off.

When you see an image that you love or one that elicits a visceral reaction, cut or tear it out. Simon Larbalestier notes, "Sometimes there is no logical reason why you are drawn to such things—they simply have a special aura that makes them compelling."

---

* Readers already familiar with the Illustrated Discovery Journal know the preparatory steps, but now we have new members of our play group and we have to get them on the same page as we are. So forgive me if this sounds familiar, but refreshers are often useful.

In the same way the creation of a collage is also fascinating since the placing of one element against another creates unexpected nuances that are otherwise unobtainable." So don't stop to analyze why you ripped out images of a flock of penguins one moment and a four-poster bed the next. The logic of it all will be revealed in the by-and-by.

You'll notice that there are nine pocket envelopes included in this journal; they are for the nine different core areas of our lives we'll be exploring together. These envelopes are the first part of your creative process; in addition to holding all your inspirational clippings, they serve as your first blank canvas. Write the categories that follow ("Authentic Style," "Entertainment," etc.) on each folder. Or print or cut out letters from magazines, ransom-note style, whatever suits the word, and your mood.

At the beginning of each section you'll find an essay to introduce the category. With any luck, my words will guide and inspire you as you begin to create your collages. But use my suggestions just to jump-start your own creative musings. As you select and gather your images, pop them into the envelope you think fits them best. The penguins could be a subconscious message concerning your spiritual journey or a relationship. Then again, you might not have a clue as to what the image means: It's a Mystery. Follow your instincts; no assessing allowed. The French painter Georges Braque confessed, "There are certain mysteries, certain secrets in my own work which even I don't understand, nor do I try to do so."

Certain mysteries are meant to be solved—such as your authentic preferences and passions. But now is not when we unravel them. Now is when we recover the mysterious parts of your authenticity. And you do that by getting reacquainted and reconnected with your imagination and intuition, the soul's telecommunication uplinks.

Think fun. Think delight. Think whoopee. This is a play date. I'm inviting you to come out (or go within!) to play with me, because our Illustrated Discovery Journals are the vehicles for us to begin playing with our Authentic Selves. Remember, girls just want to have fun—and as far as I'm concerned, we don't have nearly enough of it!

Skeptical? It's okay. Often skeptics make the best seekers. But did you know that when psychologists work with amnesiacs, one of the most effective and gentlest ways to help them remember who they are is by showing them different images and seeing which they perk up or recoil at? If you often feel like you're walking around in a strange woman's body, raising her kids and working her shift, let me say this again, so that I'm sure you understand: The only way you can go wrong with the Illustrated Discovery Journal is to think it won't work for you the way it has for thousands of other women.

But magazine and catalog pictures are just the beginning. You'll also be collecting and adding favorite quotes, sketches, greeting cards, photocopies of photographs

(you probably don't want to glue down the real thing), feature-article headlines, trave[r]
brochures, art postcards, ribbons, menus, pressed flowers, mock-ups of magnificer[t]
events you want to occur in the future—and any other darn thing you want that tri[g-]
gers a memory, whether it's past, present, or to come. The idea is to craft on these page[s]
what the poet W. H. Auden calls a map of your planet.

After you've spent a leisurely and enjoyable month gathering images, it's tim[e]
to begin creating your collages. I know you're eager, but try to resist the temptation t[o]
create nine different ones immediately.

Do only one at a time. Why? Because this is a meditative insight tool as well a[s]
a playmate, which means you want to bring your full concentration to each collage[.]
Remember that these are the illustrations of your soul's autobiography. This is the firs[t]
rough draft of your magnum opus, which is Latin for "great work," the most importan[t]
work in a person's life. As far as I'm concerned, that's discovering who we are and wh[y]
we are here at this point in eternity.

In the essays that follow throughout this Discovery Journal, I have suggeste[d]
some of my favorite collage explorations, just to get you started. But there is one cru[-]
cial collage in the excavation process that will help you get in touch with your authen[-]
tic preferences and beliefs very quickly, and I encourage you to do it in every category[.]
It's what I call a cliché collage. In filmmaking there is an expression, "stock footage[,]"
which is a collection of generic images that can be fill-ins for the real thing. For exam[-]
ple, did you ever wonder why the wild, wild west always looked the same whether it wa[s]
Gene Autry, Roy Rogers, or John Wayne riding across it? That's because behind th[e]
actors, no matter what the movie, the same scenery or stock footage was edited in[.]
Several years ago, on a trip to Four Corners in the western United States, I was amuse[d]
to discover that the expansive western landscape of my imagination actually occupie[d]
only a two-square-mile area. I could identify practically every rock.

So it is with nearly all our societal impressions and assumptions, because w[e]
have been bombarded with the same images since childhood. But these hackneye[d]
stereotypes—the blond bimbo, the finger-pointing angry deity, or the alien from oute[r]
space—are not any more real than the tumbling tumbleweeds of our childhoo[d]
Saturday-morning westerns. So we've got to get rid of them. You'll do that with th[e]
cliché collages. You know how great it feels when you clean out a closet? Wait until yo[u]
start throwing away society's images of what makes you happy.

While I have urged you not to come to any hasty conclusions or to try to ana[-]
lyze your collages as you create them, invariably as you cut and paste, an insight wil[l]
appear suddenly, a bolt of inspired reckoning or reconnection out of the blue. A reve[-]

lation that seems to have arrived in the hands of angels. "Wow," you'll say, and then forget all about it. Most of the major emotional and spiritual breakthroughs I remember have been accompanied by an insistent voice saying "Write this down." I encourage you to do the same, which is why I've included a "Notes" page at the end of each section.

I believe with all my heart that authenticity is the most personal form of worship and thanksgiving. There is no more exciting, inspiring, and important adventure that the reunion with your Self. There is no gift from Spirit greater than knowing who you are and owning her with joy and gratitude.

So get to it and have a blast!

Blessings on your courage.

Sarah Ban Breathnach

MAY 1999

THE ILLUSTRATED
DISCOVERY JOURNAL

It's been a rare year, o paper soul…
Maybe I should fold you away to pull you out again in a decade,
see whether the flowering that now seems promised, came;
see whether it was untimely frostbit, or died without fruit,
because you chart the real deeps of me.
No: I hold you a pelorous, a flexing mirror, strange quarters
for the wind of God.

—KERI HULME

AUTHENTIC STYLE

Style is something peculiar to one person; it expresses one personality and one only; it cannot be shared.

—FREYA STARK

ONE OF THE TRUTHS I LEARNED ON MY *SIMPLE Abundance* journey is that you cannot begin the search for authenticity, you cannot embark on a spiritual path within, and not see it reflected on the outside. We're talking about style, fitness, and beauty. Girl talk. Sister stuff. Soul speak. Chick concerns. The eternal question: *How do I look?*

Let's start by making a quick cliché collage. Flip through your magazines and catalogs and cut out the images that embody style to you. Think about how you'd like to look. Money is no problem. Nor are physical flaws—this collage should be your cosmic wish list. So cut out the most flattering designer clothes you want, the long legs you've yearned for, the cute, perfect nose. Select a few accessories, perhaps some shoes, and a few great haircuts. Paste them all down.

Now step back. Do any of the women in the collage resemble you? Is your body, age, shoes, bank balance, or hairstyle reflected in the ones you see there? Or does looking at the collage only remind you (as if you need it) that there's a big gap between how you want to look and how you actually do? Mine did. But instead of being depressed, I got excited. So should you. Suddenly, at least I had an inkling of what the inner woman looked like. She had been a stranger for decades, and it was wonderful to make her acquaintance.

Remember, you're hunting for your authentic style, so professional teenage waifs don't work as role models. Instead, become your own reality model. You're going to learn to dress, exercise, and style your Authentic Self. If you can learn this while enjoying both the process and the result, you'll find that you're dying to show yourself off.

Doesn't that sound great?

Yes, you think. Great. But is it possible?

I promise it is. If I made it down this road, you can too. The hard part, as always, is getting over our hang-ups. You have to turn your self-loathing into self-loving, and you have to stop the lifelong habit of denying your intrinsic beauty. So many women suffer from "looking-glass shame," which is what the English novelist Virginia Woolf called the malady of self-loathing that breaks all our hearts. Some person or event in our childhood marked us as plain, ugly, or fat, and now we have a hard time seeing our real reflection. Instead, we look at the faces and bodies in magazines and use their impossible, airbrushed comeliness to feel even worse about our own.

Women have always tried either to flee from the looking glass or to fool it. Archaeologists in Asia Minor have found the burial sites of women filled with elaborate cosmetic enhancements. It seems that the ancients too, from Egypt's first female pharaoh, Hatshepsut, to Helen of Troy, felt compelled to conceal their true images, camouflaging themselves even into the next world, comfortable neither here nor in the Hereafter with who they really were.

I don't want to carry that burden one step farther. I'm tired of spending so much energy fighting myself and avoiding mirrors. Aren't you?

Starting today, if you can't be with the body you love, be willing to love the body you're with. Declare a détente with your imperfections and lay down the brutal artillery of self-abuse—the potions, prayers, and punitive diets that bludgeon our souls. The cosmetic artifice and extreme, customized correction. I'm not suggesting that there isn't a place for hair color, makeup, and cosmetic nipping and tucking on your way to authenticity if it's going to help awaken you to your inner beauty. But I assure you that nothing will help you get over looking-glass shame if the transformation doesn't begin from within.

So let's start there.

If we are good to our bodies and spirits, our Authentic Self not only will be closer to the surface, she'll be more fun to dress. Being good to my own body always has been a tough one for me, as it is for many women. One way to nurture yourself is to take care of it. But when self-care becomes a chore, we give it up almost as soon as we start a new eating plan or exercise program.

Make a collage of the physical activities that make you feel joyous. When our bodies move and blood pumps in and out of our hearts, our physical and spiritual selves are happy to be alive. They rejoice. So even if you are adamantly opposed to the very notion of exercise, like I was, let's try to think of some way to trick your body into creative movement for a half hour a few times a week.

Perhaps you enjoy playing tennis with friends? Gardening? Walking in the beautiful park down the street? Pushing your baby on the swing (a real biceps and triceps workout)? Making love? If you have a hard time thinking of more than one or two physical pleasures that delight you, think back to your childhood. If there's an activity you used to love but gave up at some point, give it another try. The rewards are worth it.

Now that we've addressed the body and the spirit, it's time to think about what we want to wear. When you're in a department store, surrounded by a dizzying array of outfits of every color, cut, and make, how do you know which outfit expresses your authentic style? How do we know which one will be the most flattering? One thing we do know: It rarely looks as good on us as it does on the mannequin, an essential truth that can send even the strongest woman reeling.

A good place to start looking for authentic fashion clues is in your photo albums. Find the pictures that reveal what you believe is the *essential you;* you'll recognize her authentic gleam by a twinkle in the eye, a buoyant smile, the confident angle of the girl's chin. Is she sassy? That's the one. Look for photographs of you at all ages, make copies and paste them into a collage. What were you wearing? What does that indicate about who you were at the time? What were you doing? A friend's favorite picture of herself shows her just after she decided to undertake a project that had previously frightened her. After having announced that momentous and exhilarating decision at a dinner party, she looked up to find someone taking her picture. The shot now hangs on her refrigerator so she can see her powerful, beautiful Authentic Self staring back at her.

Does this sound familiar? Don't you long to revel in your own sense of majesty and importance? Don't you hunger to rekindle that deeply felt desire for stopping traffic? Why shouldn't you reclaim it?

Before your next shopping trip, this is what I want you to do. Remember the glimmer in your six- or seven- or eighteen-year-old eye, and make a collage of the type of outfits you'd love to wear if you were sure that all you'd hear would be fabulous compliments about how great you look. You're after something different, offbeat, or dramatic. After you've completed this collage, prop the book up so that you can become familiar with this showstopping woman. Now head to a thrift or vintage clothing shop and pick out one piece of clothing or an accessory that captures this secret you. For example, I adore vintage hats, especially veiled ones, and I've collected quite a few. But I had to spend some time wearing them around the house before I could feel comfortable enough to display my splendor to the world. Even then I did it in baby steps, wearing a hat out to lunch with a good friend, or when traveling among strangers. As the writer Patricia Hampl admits, "Maybe being oneself is always an acquired taste."

Another exercise that can be very revealing is to make a collage of colors that make you smile. Cut out splashes of color from magazines, or use wallpaper samples, or try to replicate your favorite hue with colored pencils or crayons. Often the colors that please you look wonderful on you even if your color chart says they shouldn't! Colors you feel passionate about somehow manage to echo your smile. Don't shy away from bright colors because you've always thought they were too much, or too attention-grabbing. If those are the colors you love, then your Authentic Self is just as bright and fabulous as they are. It took me years to realize that gold was a color I should wear. I had ignored the fact that every time I put it on, I shined.

Here are some simple questions to help you identify the external aspects of your authentic style. Are you wildly theatrical, or softly romantic? What patterns, textures, fabrics do you like? Do you have a favorite store or designer? Do you like outrageous jewelry, or small, delicate pieces? Do you enter a room quietly, but long to make a big entrance?

Okay, we're through with the warm-up collages—now you can pull out all the stops and have some fun. Create a collage celebrating your authentic style. Flip through catalogs and magazines and photo albums. Dress your Authentic Self in the colors and textures and style she craves. Maybe she looks sleek and elegant in black, or wildly festive in a South American print. Don't forget accessories. I had a fabulous time with this collage, and in the process I discovered my penchant for glamorous clothing of the twenties, thirties, and forties. Nothing gives me as much pleasure as putting together an entire outfit—complete with hat, gloves, shoes, purse—and now I mix vintage accessories with contemporary pieces. It's become my signature style.

Now that we've created expressions of our Authentic Selves, I'm afraid it's time to get practical. We need to talk about balance, and the realities of your life, and how they will affect your authentic style. Because if you've found that your clothing of choice is sequined evening gowns and Manolo Blahnik shoes and you're a working mother of two young children, you're going to have to learn to compromise a little bit. I had to compromise too: The fringe on my favorite black flapper-style dress just seems to get in the way when I'm at home writing.

The essence of discovering your authentic style, which is the external, visual expression of your Authentic Self, is finding the point of balance between how you want to look and how you do look. You have to create harmony between the reality of your daily round and your visions of grandeur. If you love the details of fashion and grooming, you are betraying your Authentic Self by running around in dirty sweatpants, no matter how little time you have in the morning. On the other hand, it is not a betrayal if you find putting on makeup boring and can't bring yourself to do it, no matter how much you admire it on others.

Ultimately, your new ideal may be your "best viable" look. For example, I have a friend who looks great with her hair cut in an intricate layered look, but it took too much attention to style it each morning. Now she has a one-length, easy-to-manage style that looks almost as good. Even better, she manages to do that one well every day, whereas the other one was hit or miss.

Final collage: a realistic depiction of your authentic style. Start slowly, gathering images that project your Authentic Self at every point during the day. What you wear when you play with the kids. When you're at the office. When you're having dinner out at a nice restaurant. When you're dancing. Even when you're sleeping. Making this collage can be incredibly freeing. Within the limits of your real daily life, you are showing how fabulous you are. At every turn, in every moment. You'll see that your style is a portrait of your Authentic Self. You are truth, inside and out. "Truth is the vital breath of Beauty," the writer Grace Aguilar wrote in 1850, "Beauty is the outward form of Truth."

When Sleeping Beauty wakes up, she is almost fifty years old. —MAXINE KUMIN

The most exhausting thing you can do is to be inauthentic.

—ANNE MORROW LINDBERGH

After a certain number of ye

r faces become our biographies. —CYNTHIA OZICK

...There is a lot of me, and all so luscious. —WALT WHITMAN

I dote on myself...

Without emotion, there is no beauty. —DIANA VREELAND

I have a sense of these buried lives striving to come out through me to express themse

Such creatures of accident are

able to a thousand deaths before we are born. But once we are here, we may create our own world, if we choose.

—MARY ANTIN

NOTES

ENTERTAINMENT

*It isn't the great big pleasures that count the most;
it's making a great deal out of the little ones.*

—JEAN WEBSTER

GENUINE PLEASURE IS ONE OF THE BEST WAYS TO
get a glimpse of your Authentic Self and bask in the warmth
of your soul's smile. Sadly, our ability to play is a natural
impulse that has atrophied. What's more, we don't recognize the
importance of playing, of relaxation, of joy. We honestly can't think
of activities that create those sensations in us. We're so tired all we can
think of is work and recuperation. But reviving yourself over the
weekend so you can just work harder next week is not relaxation.
It's survival.

Entertainment is all about pleasure. Enjoyment. Enthusiasm.
As one of my daughter's friends says, "Whatever floats your boat."
What is it that floats your boat? Do you even know where the boat is
moored? It's been too long since we've set sail on pleasurable seas.

Often, rather than concentrating on what we truly enjoy on

free evenings and weekends, we try to achieve many other social goals and meet other people's obligations. How many of your weekends turn into some sort of to-do list of social calls? Let's be honest: Many of us participate in activities because we should, because it's stylish, because our friends do, or because we are incapable of saying no.

But this purposeful pleasure deprivation leads to resentment; instead of enjoying yourself, you begin to feel sorry for yourself, put upon. Only you can free yourself from the trap of that kind of thinking. You will never begin to live joyfully until the day you stop seeing yourself as a martyr to your work, your family, or anything else in life.

The only person in all the world who can give you pleasure, or deny it, is yourself. No matter how much we love someone, the decision to experience pleasure, and to make room for it in our lives, is an internal one. If you are resistant, you could be around the most joyous people in the world and be miserable.

For your quick cliché collage, paste down your definition of "entertainment." Flip through magazines, catalogs, your local paper. Are you cutting out images of movies? Concerts? Books? Craft projects? Remember, no selection is right or wrong. You're just purging your preconceived notions of entertainment so you can open up and find out what truly is fun for you. In the following collages, you will get in touch with the activities that make your Authentic Self squeal with delight. And if you don't—keep trying. It's worth it.

Very often there is a connection between what entertained us as children and what entertains us now. Create a collage about how you played during childhood. When my brothers and sister and I were bored, we put on plays in the backyard and invited the whole neighborhood to watch. If you did the same thing, cut out a picture of a stage. Were you a master at jacks? Paste down a picture of a spiky metal jack set from a toy catalog or draw one yourself.

If you put on shows as a child, is the theater still a part of your life? If you haven't been to a play in years, buy tickets to a local production, or volunteer to work behind the scenes in set design or props. You'll be surprised at how much joy you feel when you revisit old passions as an adult. If you loved to finger-paint, perhaps your sense of play can be reawakened by working with your hands. You might enjoy tossing bread dough in the air, molding a pot, or creating jewelry out of beads you can buy at your favorite craft store.

The point of this collage is to look back at your childhood and see whether there is a connecting thread between what you enjoyed doing then and what you enjoy doing now. If there is no connecting thread, create one. Never underestimate the wisdom of your nine-year-old, hard-playing, fun-loving Authentic Self. She has much to teach you.

∽

But it isn't only the big stuff, like theater and film and crafts, that entertains us. I want you to create a collage made up of small, inexpensive, simple pleasures. Pull out your magazines, catalogs, and your photo albums. Think about pastimes that are enjoyable for you, moments when you felt very close to your Authentic Self. What were you doing? Were you standing on the beach, staring into the ocean? Taking a walk, alone or with a loved one? Maybe you love nothing better than curling up on the couch and getting lost in the latest offering of your favorite mystery writer. As you cut out and paste the images that represent these activities, be aware of the sense of pleasure stirring through your body. Jot down any realizations you experience on the "Notes" page of this chapter.

∽

Now imagine having an entire day to spend however you like—no commitments, no obligations, no duties, no dependents. Money is no concern. Hopefully, the previous collages have nudged your imagination. So create a collage of your ideal day. This day can be a combination of every activity that entertains you, or just one. You could sleep late, then go out to brunch with friends, followed by a long leisurely stroll at a flea market, followed by a movie matinee. Or you might fly to Paris on the Concorde and savor a bowl of French onion soup within sight of the Eiffel Tower. The possibilities are endless and exhilarating.

These collages will introduce a new way of thinking and perhaps a whole new subject to be explored: entertaining yourself. Not your kids or your husband or your friends. Your Self. I know this is a radical idea, maybe even a scary one. I understand. It was for me, at first, too. As strange as it might sound, most of us have to use self-discipline to learn or rediscover the activities and pastimes that truly thrill our minds, hearts, and souls. Spirit has given us the unlimited capacity for joy specifically as a balm for the stress and strain of everyday life, but only we can make sure that we take advantage of that wonderful gift.

If an all-out campaign to indulge the "hedonist" in you just doesn't feel right, don't force it. For many of us, one simple pleasure a day is the right speed for moving toward self-preservation. Just be sure to indulge in enough to rediscover the sensation of joy.

Perhaps the most important reason to play and respect your need for it is that many of the answers you're searching for in this excavation process of your Authentic Self will be found more easily at play. As William Shakespeare wrote, "I pray you...your play needs no excuse. Never excuse."

There is an applause superior to that of the multitude—one's own.

—ELIZABETH ELTON SMITH

One of the secrets of a happy li

s continuous small treats. —IRIS MURDOCH

It is in our idleness, in our dreams, that the submerged truth sometimes comes to the top. —VIRGINIA WOOLF

The material for this book was collected directly from nature at great personal risk by the author. —HELEN ROWLAND

People who keep journals have life twice. —JESSAMYN WEST

To express the emotions of life is to liv

To express the life of emotions is to make art. —JANE HEAP

NOTES

AUTHENTIC SUCCESS

Know the difference between success and fame.
Success is Mother Teresa. Fame is Madonna.

—ERMA BOMBECK

WHEN WE WERE LITTLE, REPORT CARDS FILLED out by teachers informed our parents how well we were doing in school. Whether we were good or bad, brilliant or disappointing, promising or pathetic. And from the chilling moment of comprehension that the opinions of virtual strangers could regulate the ebb and flow of approval from our parents, we were never psychologically or emotionally the same. We covered up our authentic core and quickly became our false self, a feminine chameleon able to change her appearance, personality, and style to suit the occasion or relationship.

One of the most difficult challenges we have to face and overcome on our journey to ransom back our self-worth is to make the transition from external judgment (what other people think about us) to internal acceptance (what each of us thinks about ourself). The Discovery Journal can be a wonderful tool to help.

When you think of success, who or what springs to mind? Mother Teresa or Madonna? Be honest now. Flip through magazines and catalogs. What types of images convey the idea of success to you? Cut out and paste down the images that leap out at you and symbolize success.

What have you ended up with? Images of wealth and opulence? A Mercedes, a mansion, and a stunning husband? Ads for fantastic, shimmering evening gowns? Photographs of bikini-clad women with eighteen-inch waists? A headline from *Forbes* magazine about the individual with the largest financial portfolio? A speaker standing in front of a cheering crowd? A woman relaxing in an Armani suit in her corner office, a picture of her happy, gorgeous family framed on her desk?

If your collage looks something like this, I'm not surprised. My original authentic success collage did too. We have been force-fed these images of success since birth—on television and film, on the news and in novels. They are plastered all over magazines and venerated by our celebrity-inebriated culture. Society tells us that successful people are beautiful and rich. Successful people move effortlessly up the corporate ladder. Their children are happy and adorable. Their marriages work. They have naturally high metabolisms.

Do these images bear any resemblance to you, or your life? Probably not. With any luck, they never will. Because these images are a cliché—the polar opposite of authentic success.

So go ahead, throw away the world's clichés. Tear them up into tiny pieces if you like, or use them as kindling in the fireplace. They have no place here. We're moving forward. Starting from scratch to create our own definition of authentic success.

Let's begin by distinguishing between your vision of external success and its interior reflection. Is external success the moment when your accomplishment is celebrated by the outside world? Is it when you receive the award, or the day your first short story is published? Flip through your personal photos and boxes of paper memorabilia and see if you can find Kodak moments of celebration. What about the picture of the champagne toast with your co-workers that appeared in the company newsletter last year? Peruse your collection of catalogs and magazines and think about what your external successes, past and future, might look like. Photocopy the article that was in the paper last year that had your name listed as one of the most active volunteers in the community. These are the images that belong in your external success collage.

Now wait a few days, and then return to your external success collage. How does it make you feel? What's your visceral reaction?

Make a few comments in the margin. When I looked at mine, I felt proud, but confused. While I was pleased with my many accomplishments, the moments captured in my collage were not necessarily the ones when I felt truly successful. Maybe you feel the same way. Perhaps seeing your name in the paper celebrating your community service left you feeling oddly unmoved, even though the hours you spend tutoring children or working at the safe house for battered women feel so satisfying. Does the picture of the champagne toast with your colleagues make you feel anxious?

Why is it that these moments of external success, when your friends and family are busy congratulating you and praising your accomplishments, don't always feel like success to your Authentic Self? Perhaps it's because the world insists that we collect tangible proof of achievements, something that can be cited on the grown-up's report card, the résumé or the bank application for a bigger mortgage.

Those goals—the college degree, the home, a comma in the checking account—can be genuinely gratifying if they resonate with your authentic interior vision. But often we lose sight of the activities that truly bring us joy, the intangibles that don't get publicly recognized. This next collage is about recognizing your authentic gifts—the projects that make your heart sing. If you can't think of anything in your current life that meets that description, go back to your childhood and teens. What did you love to do back then? What do you see as your natural talents—then and now? If you could have ten other career choices, what would they be? Who would you be? What activity makes you glow, makes the hours slip away?

The answers might be playing with your child, or gardening, or editing a rough piece of writing into something great. Or cooking for your family, or painting a landscape, or acting in a local theater group. Or maybe even daydreaming. Who knows, your Authentic Self might be a philosopher. Whatever these activities are, cut them out and paste them down. Don't hesitate before selecting a symbol for something you love to do simply because you don't think you're good at it or worry that someone else may think it's frivolous or unworthy. From this moment, at least on the pages of this book, nobody else's opinion counts for anything. We're reimaging success in a whole new way, remember? Keep cutting and pasting. This collage is about opening doors. Doors that you may very well have locked from the inside because you were afraid. And not of failing, either. Of succeeding.

When you're ready—and I hope it takes a while—start your final collage. Play with this one over a period of time. Be on the lookout for images, colors, smiles, journeys, and moments of work that make you happy. Select pictures of the process, of the internal moment, of the knowledge that you are using your authentic gifts and following your own path. Paste down a photo of the painting you're halfway through, or a picture of your garden in its third spring. Photocopy the two hundredth page of your four-hundred-page novel, or the title of a rewarding project at work. Select a picture of your child's face and press it into your collage with loving fingertips—here's another glorious work-in- progress.

Now, isn't this what Authentic Success really looks like?

*The real moment of success is not
the moment apparent to the crowd.*

—GEORGE BERNARD SHAW

Your first job is to get our own story straigh

—NATALIE GOLDBERG

What another would have done as well as you, do not do it. What another would have said as well as you do, do n say it. What another would have written as well, do not write it. Be faithful to that which exists nowhere but in yourself—and thus make yourself indispensable. —ANDRE GIDE

Many people are so busy knocking themselves out trying to do everything they think they should do, they never g round to what they want to do. —KATHLEEN WINSOR

Out of the strain of the Doing,

Into the peace of the Done.   —JULIA LOUISE WOODRUFF

If ambition doesn't hurt you, you haven't got it. —KATHLEEN NORRIS

If you have no anxiet

the risk you face is probably not worthy of you. Only risks you have outgrown don't frighten you. —DAVID VISCOTT

NOTES

THE HOUSE OF BELONGING

*The ideal of happiness has always taken material form
in the house, whether cottage or castle; it stands for permanence
and separation from the world.*

—SIMONE DE BEAUVOIR

ALMOST NO IMAGE HOLDS AS MUCH SWAY OVER
our romantic reveries as the dream house we will someday
buy or build. For our first cliché collage, I want you to pick
out images of the house you've always dreamed of owning. It might
be a southern mansion like Tara in *Gone with the Wind*, or possess the
sleek vision of a Frank Lloyd Wright, or it may be a small cottage with
a white picket fence. Flip quickly through real estate brochures and
magazines such as *In Style, Architectural Digest,* and *House & Garden.*
If you see a house that resembles the one in your mind's eye, put it in
the collage. It doesn't have to be a literal depiction. If you see a gin-
gerbread house in a food catalog with frosted "windows" that look
like those on your dream home, cut it out. Paste all these images down.

Step back and look at the different sides of the house you've spent your life longing for.

But is the house in this cliché collage the home your Authentic Self craves? There may be things that you've learned about yourself over the years (or perhaps in the course of using this Discovery Journal) that don't match up with the kind of house you've centered your collage around. You may have liked modern homes since you were a child, but you also know that now you prefer small rooms to large ones because of their cozy and reassuring feel. In reality, though, most modern homes are built with few internal walls and high cathedral ceilings. So perhaps a modern house is not truly the ideal home for you. You might be more comfortable in a colonial home furnished with contemporary furniture. The point of the cliché collage is to take a good look at the home you've dreamed about since you were little. You've lived several lifetimes since then, and undoubtedly you've lived in several different homes. Perhaps it's time to relinquish your fixed hold on this particular version of your dream house. It's now time to seek and find your House of Belonging.

The House of Belonging is an ancient Celtic metaphor for the human body as the earthly home for the soul; it is also used to describe the deep peace and feeling of safety, joy, and contentment found in intimate soul-friend relationships. This beautiful expression of connection is poetically explored in John O'Donohue's book *Anam Cara*. "When you learn to love and to let your self be loved, you come home to the hearth of your own spirit. You are warm and sheltered. You are completely at one in the house of your own longing and belonging."

Interior designer and author Alexandra Stoddard tells us, "Think of the inside of your house as your soul and the outside architecture as something like your bone structure, your genetic inheritance....Our true home is inside each of us, and it is your love of life that transforms your house into your home."

Since you are in the process of rediscovering your Authentic Self, don't you think it's time to re-create the image of your dream home?

For your next collage, let's decorate our House of Belonging. There are two ways you can do this. One is to make a single collage to represent the entire interior of the house. Money is no object. This is the time to pick out the furniture, curtains, knickknacks, and architectural designs you like best. Flip through home and decorating magazines, as well as wonderful catalogs like *Pottery Barn, Chambers,* and *Spiegel.* Do you like lace curtains or plain window shades? Would you like to have a fireplace in your bedroom? Should the desk where you pay the bills be made of light wood or have the heft and solidity of mission style? What fabrics do you love? Would you prefer a hard-wood floor in your kitchen or a tile one? Would you like to have built-in bookshelves in your living room? What other features would you enjoy? A scented linen drawer? A window seat in the upstairs hall? A rose-covered gazebo in the backyard?

By putting down on paper what your soul desires, you are sending out a message to the Cosmos that will, in its own time, be answered. Fifteen years ago I saw an ad in a magazine for a set of beautiful floral Ralph Lauren sheets. I loved them immediately, but was unable to afford them. It took six years before I finally bought the Ralph Lauren sheets, and I chose to decorate my bedroom around their pattern. This was a wonderful lesson in delayed gratification for me. I used the sheets for many years, and never entered my bedroom without being soothed and comforted by the sight of them.

Often, when people say that their house makes them happy, they mean that it makes them feel comfortable and content. It can be very rewarding to create a collage about what comfort means to you. Comfort is in the details: a thick down comforter on your bed, a beautiful set of china teacups, a throw rug on the floor in front of the sink. Cut out images of items that bring you comfort. It might be brightly colored pillows, a warm bathrobe, or a lamp that shines a soft golden light. Other ideas might be a roaring fire, a teakettle on the stove, or delicate curtains fluttering at the window. It can be a revelation to find that the things you value most in your home are often the small, relatively inexpensive items. Your comfort collage should help you realize not only which items you want to buy, but it should also aid you in appreciating the small pieces currently in your home that bring you great pleasure.

Another facet of our House of Belonging is the garden. Make a collage of your own secret, ideal garden. With the help of your home magazines and gardening catalogs, create a bed of flowers or vegetables that appeals to all of your senses. You can satisfy many cravings with a garden—not only a hunger for food, but a hunger for color. You can create a masterpiece of color with your garden just as much as you can with a paintbrush. Decide whether you want to focus on vegetables or flowers. Do you want to be able to feed your family from your garden, or simply your senses? What is the color scheme of your garden? What kind of flowers do you like? Brightly colored or muted? Small-budded or large? Is your secret garden neat and geometrical or wild and natural? This collage can be helpful even if you don't think you'll ever get around to growing a garden of your own. You don't need to create a garden anywhere other than on this page to learn about your Authentic Self. If you prefer an overgrown garden, usually that means you are a loose, creative spirit, whereas if you prefer a classically English, tailored garden, your temperament might be more organized and methodical.

Another collage that's useful for creating your House of Belonging is one that celebrates color. I know that you already made a color collage in "Authentic Style," but this is different. The colors you choose to wear are often the very opposite of the colors you'd choose to live with. I can't wear the color yellow because it makes me look sallow, but for years I adored the pale yellow of my living room walls. You might like to wear bright red, yet not want to paint your bedroom that color. As you flip through your magazines and catalogs, think about the colors you want in your House of Belonging. What color rugs, walls, plates, towels, curtains? Cut out any color that elicits a visceral response in you. For instance, I once decorated an entire room around the color of a peach found in a seed catalog because its rich tone excited me so much. On our journey to authenticity, once we learn to open our eyes, inspiration is literally everywhere. When you look at your finished collage, you might find that neutral colors soothe and please you. Or you might be surprised to find the page dominated by bright yellows and blues. Just be open to the truths you discover in these pages.

One of the great joys of living in your House of Belonging is inviting your friends and loved ones to visit. Think about holding the perfect dinner party in your home, and then create a collage around that idea. Your collage should show the setup of your dining room, where the party will be held. Cut a beautiful dining room table out of one catalog and chairs out of another. Select and hang an elegant crystal chandelier, or minimalist sconces, or whatever lighting makes you light up. When you run across a flower arrangement you think is gorgeous, cut it out and paste it onto the center of your collage table. Pick out the most beautiful china pattern you can find and paste it around the table. Then think about what your favorite comfort foods are. Paste down turkey and mashed potatoes, or fettucine Alfredo, or fried chicken and corn on the cob. Do you like cheesecake for dessert? Key lime pie? Chocolate mousse? Load your collage table with good food until its legs sag under the weight. Isn't this fun? This was how Victorian children created their playhouses. Step back and look at your own playhouse. Doesn't its very style, and your longing for it, give you great pleasure? Now imagine how wonderful it will be when the time arrives, and the hostess, your Authentic Self, answers the door, making this party a reality.

Building the House of Belonging is the soul's commitment to living a passionate life; your Authentic Self is the architect.

You must be courageous to create and live in your House of Belonging. But you are, or you wouldn't be on this journey. Remember, your approach doesn't have to be all or nothing. If money or fear stands in your way, keep dreaming and bide your time. Even if you can't move into the antebellum southern mansion of your dreams, perhaps you can decorate your bedroom with that feeling. Think small. Think do-able. Baby steps will still get you there. The blueprints of your House of Belonging exist as spiritual energy and hover over your head, ready, when you are, to be pulled down from Heaven to shelter your soul on Earth. Each day, as Emily Dickinson says, you "dwell in possibility." You must believe this, because it's true.

There are homes you run from, and homes you run to.

—LAURA CUNNINGHAM

I have no home but me. —ANNE TRUITT

Peace— that was the other name for home.   —KATHLEEN NORRIS

A house is no home unless it contains food and fire for the mind as well as for the body. —MARGARET FULLER

I had to leave home, so I cou

…find myself, find my own intrinsic nature buried under the personality that had been imposed on me.

—GLORIA ANZALDÚA

Emily Dickinson never left her house after the age of thirty. Why should she leave? She was reinventi the world, she needed to stay in one place. —JEAN HOUSTON

NOTES

RETURN TO SELF

What a desire! ... To live in peace with that word:
Myself.

—SYLVIA ASHTON-WARNER

I don't suppose anyone has called you self-centered recently. Why would they? Can you even remember the last time you considered your preference before anyone else's? Didn't think so. Well, you're not alone.

Most women recoil from the thought of personal descriptions that include the word *self*, which is too bad because this self-defeating modesty eliminates a lot of flattering adjectives: self-poised, self-assured, self-confident. So why do you self-consciously shrink from self-admiration?

Probably because ever since your hand was slapped as you reached for the last cookie on the plate all those years ago, you've viewed satisfying your healthy wants and lusty needs as shameful and selfish. But now that you're grown up and ready to rediscover how glorious you really are, it's time to realize that the cheeks that once burned with embarrassment now radiate with the vibrant glow of a self-possessed woman.

One way we learn how to mask our self-loathing is by making sure that everyone else on the planet is happy. That's why you know how to please, cajole, comfort, and delight your parents, partners, friends, boss, or children and haven't a clue how to give Guess Who a moment of self-pleasure.

Which is how you die from self-pity, and believe me, it's not a pretty sight.

But starting now, you're going to change all that. It takes courage, but you're ready.

Can you be honest about how you see yourself? About what you see in the mirror on your worst days? I'm serious here. It's time to take the kid gloves off. Do you sometimes whisper negative comments at your reflection? Here's your chance to shout them. Any vestige of self-loathing you have hidden in the secret cavity of your heart—now's the time to exorcise it. "Loathe?" you might ask nervously. "That's a strong word. I don't like some things about myself, sure, but I wouldn't say I loathe myself." Sure you do. Because, unfortunately, that's how most women feel deep inside. So let's just admit it, so we can finally get over it.

Loathing is a grief that has festered, the rampant infection of self-pity. To loathe something or someone is to detest with disgust and intolerance. How do we loathe ourselves? Let me count the ways: reasons that have nothing to do with our appearance, age, or weight. Some of the world's most famous beauties can't stand the sight of themselves.

For our throwaway collage, you're going to select images that show the way you see yourself in the mirror. Exaggerate, be honest, err on the side of grotesque. Cut and paste with vigor. Draw on the energy of your self-loathing. Show what you really, deep down, think of your appearance. If you hate your hair, cut out the ugliest haircuts you can find in your array of catalogs and magazines. If you feel overweight, find a picture of a huge naked woman and paste it down. Hate your upper arms and refuse to wear sleeveless dresses? Flip through your magazines and select the jiggliest pair of upper arms you can find. Your thighs are the bane of your existence? Your nose is too big? Move quickly through your magazines and catalogs and pull out the biggest and the fattest and gleefully paste them down onto your collage. Come on, girlfriend, get it all out.

When you're finished, take a good look at the collage. Do you, honestly, see yourself anywhere on that page? No, of course not. What you're looking at is a picture of your self-loathing. You are not your self-loathing. Your Authentic Self, body or soul, is nowhere to be found in that collage. Thank God!

Now that you can finally see what the ugly disease of self-loathing looks like, you can perform an emotional exorcism. Tear up your cliché collage. Destroy every last vestige of your self-loathing. Bid it farewell. You are way too fabulous to be dismissed, imprisoned, or held back by hallucinations of inconsequence. Tell your self-loathing that you're moving on, and that you're traveling light this time. You've got no room for those kinds of destructive forces, those cellulite-ridden images. Good-bye and good riddance.

Do you feel cleaner? Perhaps lighter? Ready for a fresh start? Good. It's about time.

Now I want you to make a collage that shows where you stand in the scheme of your own life. What do I mean? I mean we need to take a look at what makes up our daily life. Driving the kids to and from school? Cooking meals? Staying late at work to finish a project? Talking to your husband about his day? Paying bills? Gardening? Finding other people's hats, gloves, business folders? Vacuuming? To start the collage, select a picture of yourself and photocopy it. Then peruse your magazines and catalogs and cut out symbols for the activities and demands that fill your days. Cut out a picture of someone who looks like or reminds you of your boss. Choose a picture of dirty dishes to represent the time after dinner you spend cleaning up. Find a picture of a car full of kids, or a picture of the nursing home where you visit your mother. Now, without stopping to think, paste these images and the photograph of yourself into a collage.

Step back. What do you see? Where do you physically fall in the collage? Are you pushed off to one corner? This might mean that you don't feel like the main character in your own life, or that you are ignoring your Authentic Self because of the overwhelming demands on your time and energy. This might also be true if the picture of you in the collage is smaller than the other images. Does the picture of your kids, or your boss, loom over your tiny figure? Your subconscious is telling you that you're giving too much, and not getting enough back. You must start creating balances of time and attention in your daily round that are true and authentic, choices that will restore harmony to your simply abundant life.

So how do you learn to develop a finely honed sense of self-worth? By giving thanks for your authenticity, even if the world calls it self-worship. What makes the blood rush to your head, your heart skip a beat, your knees shaky, and your soul sigh?

When you can answer these questions, it's time to start your final collage. Use this one to revel in the self you have returned to. The Self you have committed to indulge in, fight for, and love—truly, madly, deeply. Celebrating your truth, passion, and originality—your authenticity—is long overdue. Go through your scrapbooks and select the prettiest picture of yourself. Copy the photograph and paste it into the center of your collage page. Smile back at yourself. Now cut an array of adjectives out of magazines, the newspaper, and catalogs. Select the adjectives that describe you, cut them out, and paste them around your picture. Maybe you selected words like *fun, adventurous, domestic, loving, fabulous.* But what about *glamorous, sexy,* or *mysterious?* Here's permission to go over the top. Be honest. Be kind. Be inventive. Select every phrase you've always and forever wanted to hear other people say about you. Let your light shine and your authentic voice roar and your smile envelope the room. For the first time, toots, make an entrance into your own life.

Just remember, when someone else calls what you're doing self-indulgent, wear the biggest, smuggest grin you've got, because you know that it's actually self-preservation. And don't forget to thank them for the compliment.

*Nobody knows what I am trying to do
but I do and I know when I succeed.*

—GERTRUDE STEIN

Like any art, the creation of self is both natural ar

seemingly impossible. It requires training as well as magic.

—HOLLY NEAR

The greatest possession is Self-possession

—ETHEL WATTS MUMFORD

The personal, if it is deep enough, becomes universal, mythical, symbolic. —ANAÏS NIN

I've never quite believed that one chance is all I get. —ANNE TYLER

nd you either wear them with style all your life, or else you

go dowdy to the grave.   —DOROTHY PARKER

I'm not ashamed of what I've had, and I'm not sad becau

I love my past. I love my present.

have it no longer. —COLETTE

NOTES

MYSTERY

*It began in mystery, and it will end in mystery
but what a savage and beautiful country
lies in between.*

—DIANE ACKERMAN

D O YOU EVER TAKE TIME OUT FROM YOUR RATIONAL, problem-solving mind-set to experience the wonder of the universe? The complexity of daily life almost demands that we spend a great deal of our mental energy in a practical, thinking mode. In fact, we often train ourselves to ignore our instincts and deny our emotions in order to be "objective" and "logical." But there are secrets of the human experience, as well as of the authentic journey, that are revealed or understood *only* by our right-brained, instinctual mind. A business colleague once complimented me on my uncanny way to think my way through even the most difficult conundrum, but I had to correct him. I don't think, I *feel* my way through the maze of mystery. Each day we are invited to experience the wonders of our beating pulse, but we have to be willing to open up, to let go, and leap toward the knowable but unthinkable, in a word, *life*.

One way to open yourself up to authentic mysteries is to look at the things that you love. How can we explain our love for certain things, our "favorite things," as the song goes? Why have you kept that old record of bagpipe music? Your collection of old coins? This length of Victorian lace? This picture of a sand dune? Why do you sigh when you see this photo of a glossy red-haired Irish setter?

One of my friends is completely intrigued by how ancient cultures managed to move huge stones. All she has to do is watch a *National Geographic* television special on the building of Stonehenge, the Easter Island gods, the pyramids, or Incan cities to experience a special rapture. Another friend is fascinated with Aboriginal art; she claims she could stare at its abstract designs forever and never get bored. One of my odd passions is collecting vintage B movie posters celebrating female prowess, such as *The Astounding She-Monster* or *The Wasp Woman*—A Beautiful Woman by Day, a Lusting Queen Wasp by Night. My walls attest to the fact that I can't get enough of them. Go figure.

But let's not try to explain these things; let's celebrate them in a collage. Flip through your magazines and catalogs looking for images that represent your quirky interests. Maybe you've always been fascinated by the space program; cut out a picture of a rocket. Perhaps you've watched every documentary and read every book you could get your hands on about the opera diva Maria Callas; find a photograph of her. Paste these pictures down on the page. Wonder at the places your soul feels at home and the people with whom your Authentic Self communes.

Anything that takes us out of ourselves, that lets us feel the wonder of life or helps us feel connected to other times or places, should have an important place in our lives, and we should treat this mystery with respect. Perhaps you've always thought that your fascination with the space program was a little silly and impractical because you're an accountant, not an astronaut. You think that space study has no place in your daily life or your future. But you know what? Who cares if it's not practical? It's essential. The topics that enthrall you offer immediate opportunities to access your Authentic Self. The important point isn't why you're curious, but simply that you are.

While you're still shaking your head over the mysteries of your first collage, let's start a second one. This is, after all, a hands-on exploration of your Authentic Self;

in some ways we never get a closer look at our soul than through our mysteries. Look through all the collages you've already made in this Discovery Journal. Do any of the folders still have pictures in them? Images that didn't make it onto one collage or another because they just didn't seem to fit? Pictures that made you wonder why you cut them out in the first place? Well, here's where they belong. I want you to make a collage out of these misfit images. Don't let it bother you if you're pasting a photograph of a one-hundred-year-old land tortoise beside a Picasso nude. Don't try to understand why you cut out these pictures. So what if you usually aren't a fan of abstract art, or, for that matter, reptiles. There are hidden truths about your Authentic Self buried in this collage. When you've pasted down all your leftover images, put the collage away in a drawer. Resist looking at it for as long as possible. When you do return to it, regard the mysteries of your Authentic Self with a sense of wonder and celebration. Don't try too hard to make sense of what you see. Instead, listen to the subtle nuances. There are personal prompts in those pictures. Follow them back to your future.

The choreographer Martha Graham always urged her dancers to "keep the channel open" to the unexpected. "There is a vitality, an energy, a quickening that is translated through you into action." We cannot understand the mystery of life, of energy. All we can do is remain open to it, to clear the way for it, and then let it move through us.

How can you make room in your home and in your heart and mind for new thoughts, new ideas, new people, and a new appreciation for those already in your life? Let your Authentic Self count the ways, then cut and paste them down on the page.

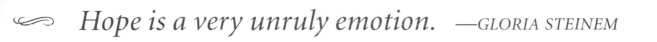

Hope is a very unruly emotion. —GLORIA STEINEM

What do you plan to do with your own wild and precious life? —MARY OLIVER

Everything in life that we really accept undergoes a change. —KATHERINE MANSFIELD

Transforming is not lying. —RAINER MARIA RILKE

...he moments of wholeness and totality of the personality.

—ANAÏS NIN

if we don't find it, we become it. —JESSAMYN WEST

NOTES

SACRED CONNECTIONS

Each relationship you have with another person reflects the relationship you have with yourself.

—ALICE DEVILLE

In our most precious relationships, we trust the other person enough to reveal our innermost selves. And we provide that safety, compassion, and acceptance for others too. But can we do that for ourselves? Can we love ourselves truly, madly, and deeply? Unfortunately, for many women the answer is no. It was for me too. But I have come to the joyful awareness, as will you, that the journey to authenticity is the greatest romance of your life.

Make a list of the key relationships in your life. You may have many, or just a few. Are you a daughter, mother, sister, wife, friend, lover? By the definition listed above, all these relationships may not feel precious, but, like it or not, they reflect the relationship we have with our Selves. By looking at your relationships through collage, you will visually discover where you stand in your relationships, and where you want them to go.

Every moment of every day, consciously, or unconsciously, we all seek *our people,* or hide from *our familiars.*

Our people should never be confused with *our familiars.* Unfortunately, we mix up the two all the time, which causes us enormous emotional distress and disillusionment. Our people are our spiritual family, the kith, kin, and kindred spirits we've unconditionally loved and been loved by since the beginning of time. Sometimes we're connected by blood and lineage. But not always.

Our familiars are those individuals whose lives intersect with ours in order to play a role crucial in helping us manifest our Divine Destiny. They can be in our lives for an hour or for what seems like an eternity—however long it takes for us to "get it," whatever life lesson the "it" may be.

Seeking the truth in relationships is scary. Take a careful look at your list. Which of these individuals represent your own inner circle—your people—the friends of your soul with whom you truly belong and feel safe? The ones with whom you feel that your Authentic Self can emerge, be appreciated, and be loved? Which family members and friends have cared about you, stood by you during difficult days, and were genuinely happy to see you flourish? These are your sacred connections.

Consider the different ways you feel about the people in your life. Some we are drawn to almost instantly. Love at first sight, for example, is a wondrous, exhilarating, and amazing sensation that many of us have experienced.

There is also such a thing as friendship at first sight. You meet someone at a party, and you immediately enjoy the way they naturally include you in the conversation. You see a new employee stand up to the boss, and admire his or her spunkiness right away. Often such connections are very real and very deep; in fact most of my closest friends are people with whom I had an almost instant sense of ease and delight.

The Irish writer John O'Donohue reminds us that "the real mirror of your life and soul is your true friend. A friend helps you to glimpse who you really are and what you are doing here."

You can learn a tremendous amount about your Authentic Self from your soul-friends, both passionate and platonic. The psychologist Carl Jung believed that "the meeting of two personalities is like the contact of two chemical substances: If there is any reaction, both are transformed." A soul-friend is someone who not only sees the real you, but helps you to see her as well.

Maybe the key relationships on your list don't meet your soulful criteria at this point in time. Maybe they never did. Maybe sacred connection is the last phrase that comes to mind when thinking about them. That's all right. Perhaps a few relationships have fallen off track due to neglect, or maybe one of you changed and grew without alerting the other. Your Discovery Journal can be a wonderful place to face the truths about your relationships and to consider their right role—at this moment in time—on your lifelong journey to Wholeness.

Select photographs of the people you love and make photocopies of them. Or sketch them. Or draw a symbol that represents them. Pick one relationship you are ready to learn more about, and dwell on it while you search through your magazines and catalogs for scenes, images, or written words that you feel are connected in some way to that person. Go through your photographs too, and photocopy any pictures that make you think about that individual, even if he or she isn't in the picture. Perhaps you'll stumble across a photograph from a time when the relationship was at its best, a time that makes you smile to remember.

When your envelope is full (and I like to gather a lot of images), you're ready to make a collage. When your collage is complete, put it aside and wait three or four days before you look at it again. And when you do return to it, don't worry if all you see in your collage is a confusing jumble of images. The meaning behind your collage will soon emerge—you just have to know what you're looking for.

First of all, study the color scheme of the collage. Is it made up of bright, positive, pleasant colors? Or is the overtone dark and dreary? Next, check for symbols. Is there a picture of a cliff or a high diving board? That might mean your relationship is at a crisis point and needs to move to a new level. I once made a relationship collage that had a picture of a tiny mouse in one corner and a powerful roaring lion in the other. When I looked at the collage I realized that I was the mouse in this particular relationship, and that I needed to shift the balance of power with my friend. I needed to approach him with greater courage and confidence. I did, and, soon after, the relationship ended. I wasn't the mouse after all.

Now that you have at least thought about making collages for all the key relationships in your life, I want you to try to wrap your mind and heart around a new subject for your Discovery Journal. This exercise may feel scary to you, but that's because it will open your heart a little wider than it's accustomed to. I'm pushing you gently past your comfort zone, but you're not alone. And I promise you the risk is worth it. We fear the most those things we can't see.

I want you to begin an envelope for your ideal love relationship: *the Other*—your soul mate. If you're married (even if you're content), don't let your mind be immediately drawn to your life with your husband. You're going to create a separate collage to explore your marriage. This is different. Dare yourself to imagine the love life you deserve. The romance. The partnership. The dance between your soul and another's. Flip through magazines with your heart pounding; whip yourself into a romantic reverie thinking of this growing, dynamic, loving, sacred connection.

When you've completed the collage of your ideal love relationship, make one about your marriage or long-standing domestic arrangement. Now compare the two collages, but don't feel despair or disappointment if they bear little resemblance to each other. Instead, feel empowered. Study the two collages: one ideal, one reality. Let the energy you feel when you look at your ideal-relationship collage elicit ideas about how you can make your current love relationship more ideal. There may be a surprising number of elements from the ideal relationship that can be integrated into your current one. Build a spiritual, psychological, and emotional bridge between the two.

It may be, however, that the gap appears too large to close, and you don't see any way to turn the relationship you're in into your ideal relationship. If this is the case, then your collage probably confirmed for you a truth you have known on a deep level for some time.

Don't blame yourself if you're not ready to make a collage about all the key relationships in your life. That's perfectly fine. You may not be ready to plumb your relationship with your mother, for example, or to look at the state of chilliness between you and your sister. You are busy gathering strength deep inside, gearing up for that future journey. You will be ready someday. Perhaps soon. In the meantime, you're strengthening your heart every time you work with your Discovery Journal. Think of your sessions as emotional cardio workouts.

It is also helpful to look at other types of relationships in your life, especially at the ones you have with your familiars. There are many lessons we can learn from people who are not soul-friends, and even from those we would hesitate to call friends at all. Perhaps these folks reflect aspects of our own personalities that we'd rather ignore. You might avoid the woman at your child's school who is forever gossiping, yet you find yourself spreading harmless rumors more than you'd like. Sometimes it's easy to see the similarities, and sometimes the parallels are less obvious. But when we look at even the most stressful relationship in this light, we can learn lessons that are very valuable in excavating our Authentic Self.

On the flip side, I have also learned a lot by allowing myself to enjoy people I never expected to like. On one memorable occasion, I was absolutely repulsed by an obnoxiously loud, laughing-too-hard man on the opposite side of a cocktail party I was attending. When a group of us decided to move on to a restaurant for dinner, I was miffed to discover that he was joining us, and dismayed when I ended up sitting next to him. Since I could not have cared less about his opinion of me, I answered his efforts at conversation by sassing him back with cheeky banter. To my great surprise, he gave as good as he got, and at one point we both began laughing. It was the beginning of a wonderful friendship full of much good humor and playfulness.

You might consider making a collage based on your relationship with one or more of the people you deal with peripherally in your daily life. Maybe the crabby postman you encounter on your lunch break every day. Or the woman in the PTA who speaks to you in that condescending manner. What's this all about?

You have nothing to lose by starting a new envelope. It's another way to look at yourself. Another mirror to pull out and use to catch a peek at one of the abundant, fascinating angles of your Authentic Self. Your relationship collages are deep, still pools that hide much emotion and much truth. I know that my attempts have made me laugh and cry and have inevitably changed the way I deal with the people in my life.

It will do the same for you.

The plots of God and Love are one and the same thing. —NIALL WILLIAMS

Ah, the relationships we get in

just to get out of the ones we are not brave enough to say are over. —JULIA PHILLIPS

No soul is desolate as long as there is a human being for whom it can feel trust and reverence. —GEORGE ELIOT

I can always be distracted by love, *but eventually I get horny for my creativity.* —GILDA RADNER

I have noticed before that there is a category of acquaintanceship that is not friendship or business or romance, but speculatio *ascination.* —JANE SMILEY

One hardly dares to say that love is the core of the relationship, though love is sought for and created in a relationship; love i

...ather the marvel when it is there, but it is not always there,

and to know another and to be known by another—that is everything.

—FLORIDA SCOTT-MAXWELL

NOTES

SPIRITUAL JOURNEY

*The spiritual journey is one of continually falling on your face,
getting up, brushing yourself off, looking sheepishly at God,
and taking another step.*

—AUROBINDO

WHAT COMES TO MIND WHEN YOU HEAR THE
phrase "spiritual journey"? Many people immediately
think of difficult lessons, painful realizations, heartbreaking
sacrifices, or the frustrations and abject loneliness of unanswered
prayers—"talking to the ceiling," as one friend used to put it.

While it's certainly true that some of the lessons we learn in life
come wrapped up in emotions, situations, and choices that are difficult
to face, one of the great blessings for me on the *Simple Abundance*
journey was the staggering realization that it's also possible to learn
our life lessons through joy. If we're ready. If we ask. Although I never
used to recognize such moments as milestones on my spiritual exploration, I now realize that some exquisite exchanges of unconditional

love and uncontrollable laughter between myself and my daughter, for example, have gifted me with many of the most "spiritual" moments of my life.

What does the word *sacred* mean to you? Have you ever felt a moment of Divine Grace? Was it in a church or temple? Were you singing hymns or saying prayers? Or were you in a field when the sun hit the grass at just the right angle? Did you feel strange that *this* was where you felt evidence of a Higher Power? For many people, organized religion doesn't provide the comfortable route to finding their God. If that's the case for you, do you feel guilty?

When we begin the excavation process of our personal beliefs, the first thing we have to do is reconsider all our previous conceptions of spirituality. This can be accomplished with a quick cliché collage. Pull out your magazines and catalogs and, for this subject, any illustrated books on religion you can get. Scan the pages for images that symbolize God or religion to you. Photocopy the images in the book, and cut or copy ones from the periodicals. Draw any of the symbols you can't find in print. Think back in time, and try to remember how you pictured God while you were sitting in religious instruction as a child, or when you were at home with your parents. This collage explores the spiritual images you've unconsciously held on to for all these years.

Perhaps your collage has pictures of benevolent saints, heavy wooden crucifixes, or a depiction of a red-hot, burning hell. Mine did. You might visualize Moses receiving the Ten Commandments, Siddhartha sitting at the base of a banyan tree before he reached enlightenment and became Buddha, red and gilt altars laden with food and incense, or the onion-shaped domes of a mosque.

Whether you have continued with the religion of your childhood or not, these images are most likely very vivid to you. The image we have of Spirit is deeply rooted in our childhood. For example, I was raised with the idea of a punishing God, a God who looked only at my sins and never at my good points. I was constantly afraid of committing sins, knowingly or unwittingly. I knew that some indescribable but very bad things would happen if I did sin, and, worse yet, that sinning would make me a bad person.

I looked at God this way for years, because that was how my parents saw him. One of my closest friends also faced this dilemma. She believed that because she felt so shut down in church, she somehow wasn't "good enough for God." Eventually she realized she was transferring the family dynamics she learned as a child dealing with her parents, and applying those same "rules" to her relationship to God. When we talked about it, I was struck by how insightful she was. Most of us, if we grew up feeling that love had to be earned, or that mistakes made us unlovable, find it hard to accept the unconditional love available to us from our Higher Power.

To find this greater truth about God, Spirit, and the sacred, we must often set aside the limiting impressions from our childhood. In many instances these images of fear only serve to hold us back in our search for authentic spirituality. If you transpose the *a* and *c* in *sacred,* you get the word *scared.* Fear is the most common roadblock in the search for a Higher Power. The images we clung to terrified us, so we abandoned the search altogether. Well, we're here to resume the search, so toss the cliché collage aside. Open up your mind and heart to a concept of Spirit who looks out for us, loves us, sheds light on our path, and wants nothing less for us than unconditional happiness.

Now, I want you to create a collage of your ideal representation of Spirit. In your magazines and journals, look for expressions of faith, kindness, and compassion. Look for smiles and a hand to guide you. Perhaps you cut out a picture of a dancer because of her beauty and grace. Another idea is to paste down several adjectives that describe God to you. You might also sketch the God you see in your mind's eye. Perhaps your ideal God is a black woman, or the quirky array of gods and goddesses the Greeks and Romans worshiped. There is no right or wrong in this collage. It is merely an authentic invitation to view ancient truth with fresh eyes.

I know that spirituality is a tough subject to make visual, but try, because thinking about God in this searching manner is a way of reaching out to the Divine. And, in my experience, when you ask for spiritual help, it will appear. It won't arrive unbidden, but you should expect it in any form.

Think about the images that induce a sense of reverence. Pull out your scissors, your magazines, and your photo albums. Think, as you flip past the images, of the moments in your life when you have looked at someone, or something, and stopped in your tracks, enveloped by the glow of the sacred. You might cut out a picture of a mother nursing her infant, or of a family sitting down to a home-cooked meal, or of the face of a laughing child. Perhaps a beautiful sunrise is sacred to you, or the look of your garden at a certain time of day. Visualize what the sacred site of your soul looks like. It could be anything: It is everything beautiful. I have discovered beauty in many spiritual paths. Now I realize that my authenticity brings them all together. As the poet Ntozake Shange discovered, "I found god in myself / and I loved her / I loved her fiercely."

So can you.

Act, and God will act. —JOAN OF ARC

I learned to think of God as a woman

and by that simple experience I discovered I could begin

think of God. —JANE O'REILLY

How can God direct our steps if we're not taking any?

—SARAH LEAH GRAFSTEIN

One cannot expect to be conscious of God's presence when one has only a bowing acquaintance with Him.

—*MADAME CHIANG KAI-SHEK*

Why is it when we talk to God we ar

said to be praying and when God talks to us we're said to be schizophrenic? —LILY TOMLIN

thrusts the thing we have prayed for in our face, A gauntlet with a gift in it. —ELIZABETH BARRETT BROWNING

NOTES

SOMEDAY

*Someday perhaps the inner light will shine forth from us,
and then we shall need no other light.*

—PIERRE SIMON DE LAPLACE

WHAT DO YOU DREAM OF DOING SOMEDAY? Writing a novel? Producing a movie? Living in an artist's loft? Driving cross-country? Owning a vineyard? We all have daydreams we cling to, even though we often wonder if we'll ever fulfill them. I call these luscious flights of fancy "somedays." They provide a revealing glimpse of an Authentic Self who rarely conjures up a fantasy not worth pursuing.

Your "someday" folder is the place to collect all those ads and mailings you've put aside for Far East adventures, New England Victorian-inn sojourns, tennis camp, and yoga classes. Sort through your collection of "someday" clippings as if you were a detective. There's a reason you've cut out seven different advertisements for health spas around the world. What might it be?

"Unfulfilled dreams are dangerous forces," cautioned the Victorian writer and educator Sarah Tarleton Colvin. So it's important to distinguish between "somedays" that are cherished, unpursued passions that excite and enrich you just to think about, and ones that are dreams fabricated by your public persona to enhance your image. These are the truly dangerous forces that have us wasting half our lives chasing other people's dreams.

When I see various depictions of the pyramids and an ad for a trip up the Nile in my own "someday" folder, I know with a wonderful assurance (which allows delayed gratification to become all it's cracked up to be) that I will go to Egypt someday. Those pyramids have been plastered on the pages of my Discovery Journal for so many years that the edges are yellowed with yearning. Vivid daydreams can exist only so long on the interior landscape of longing before they must burst, fully grown, to be acted upon.

On the other hand, I may be content simply to fantasize about opening my own vintage clothing store. This is a "someday" dream of mine that is lovely to contemplate, but I don't feel the pressing need to make it real. I find that I'm happy enough to patronize the fabulous shops run by other women who, unlike me, couldn't resist the pull to make their own vintage clothing shop dreams come true.

One way to distinguish a goal from a "someday" is to ask yourself a simple question: If money and other people's obligations were not a consideration, would you jump out of bed tomorrow morning and go do it? I suggest you limit yourself to just five of these "somedays." More than that and you're just casting your dreams adrift in the riptides of indecision and procrastination.

Your "somedays" may be symbolic, a message from your Authentic Self to your subconscious. Study them, perhaps even "translate" them. Ask yourself if they contain a message, and if so, what it is. You long to scale Mount Everest? Okay, have you ever been on a five-mile mountain hike? Rock climbed at the gym? No? Then this "someday" could be indicating a need for a slice of exotica, which might be sated by treating yourself to dinner at that new Afghani restaurant that just opened up in your neighborhood. Often I have found that after I've translated their encoded message, these "somedays" lose their urgency because I've been soothed in another unexpected, but no less palpable, way.

There is still another type of "someday" that hovers on the horizon of our feverish brains: *Phantoms of the Obligation.* These are the "somedays" you mutter to yourself while getting dressed in the morning, or on your way to work. Often these phantoms of derision and decision are concerns that we carry around in our backpack of guilt every day. "Someday I will lose ten pounds." "Someday my husband and I will go to counseling and resolve this issue." "Someday I will be home more with the kids." "Someday I'll go to the gym." "Someday I'll stand up to my boss." "Someday I'll get a decent haircut."

❧

Make a collage out of images that express your guilt-ridden, pain-sodden "somedays." Cut out a picture of an overweight woman to represent the pounds you want to lose. Take a Polaroid of the living room that needs to be redecorated so badly that you wince every time you pass its doorway. Cut out of a magazine a picture of a man and woman in deep conversation, to represent the problems you and your husband need to work on together. Find a picture of a little girl doing her homework with her mother. Cut out an ad for gym membership, and a photograph of someone having a bad-hair day. As you flip through your magazines and catalogs, cut out every image that makes you cringe and pledge, *Someday, I will…*

But actually you won't, unless this someday is soul driven. Consider this collage an exorcism. When you've plastered a good percentage of your guilt onto the page, step back and take a look. This is a depiction of blame and the unwieldy discomfort of culpability you carry around every day of your life. Negative energy. No fun. Now that you can see this hodgepodge of contrition spread out before you, can you knock a few things off the list? Have you been reproaching yourself for years about losing those ten extra pounds? Well, maybe it's time either to accept your body for what it is or to change your eating and exercising habits. Make a choice—now—and move on. These guilty "somedays" are just weighing you down, and psychic pounds register more on serenity's scale than fat or muscle. If there's an image on the collage that leaps out at you, or appears more than once, perhaps you should address that "someday" and make a conscious choice to stop nagging yourself about the others. Ask the beautiful woman at the office whom you've always admired from afar where she gets her hair cut, and make an appointment there for yourself. Place a call to a therapist for you and your husband, then show up, even if you go alone. Resolve not to let the remaining phantom "somedays" rob you of any more time, creative energy, or emotion. You're going to need them for all of life's good stuff.

That's why it's fun to create positive "someday" collages. Maybe one could plan the trips on the horizon of your fabulous future, or a career path, or a fantasy, such as becoming a country-and-western Dixie chick. Three women did it and are having a ball. Who's to say?

The final category of "somedays" is do-able this week. This collage is pure pleasure that does not have to be postponed—a celebration of small moments and badly needed self-nurturing. I know that, somewhere in the back of your brain, there's a list of things you think, wistfully, that you'd really like to get to someday. Like going to the stationery store, selecting a beautiful photo album, and putting your photographs into it with labels and dates. Lining your dresser drawers with beautiful scented linen paper, so that every time you reach for a bra, the fragrance and sublime order of the drawer makes you smile. Framing the finger-painting efforts of your toddler. Planting a kitchen herb garden. Preparing one of the intricate recipes in your French cookbook.

Create a collage of your wonderful, delicate "somedays." These small, ephemeral, achievable moments that enfold and enwrap you in contentment. It may be years before you have the time or money to achieve the "somedays" of our first collage. But even if a ride across the desert on a camel isn't in your near future, can you clear a few hours on a Saturday to visit a local museum's Egyptian collection? Even if you live in an apartment and can only dream about that wildflower garden, why not plant a few pots of herbs to adorn your kitchen windowsill? Look at your finished collage (wasn't it fun to make?) and pick out one or two activities you can start soon. Often these small, nurturing moments are wants that we don't express, even to ourselves, because we're so convinced that there's no time; it's just not possible. But by looking at your collage and realizing how much joy and self-pleasure there is to be found in the overlooked, you ransom back a portion of your lost heart and honor those long-overdue IOUs. As Margaret Bonnano tells us, "It is only possible to live happily ever after on a day-to-day basis."

And if you do, you'll discover that "someday" is closer than you think.

*I am extraordinarily patient, provided I
get my own way in the end.*

—MARGARET THATCHER

Neglecting small things because one wishes to do great things is the excuse of the faint-hearted. —ALEXANDRA DAVID-NEEL

woman, but an advanced old woman is uncontrollable by any earthly force. —DOROTHY L. SAYERS

A strong woman is a woman who loves strongly and weeps strongly and is strongly terrified and has strong needs. —MARGE PIERCY

I have been absolutely terrified every moment of my life and I've never let it keep me from doing a single thing

I wanted to do. —GEORGIA O'KEEFFE

Only one thin

is more frightening than speaking your truth. And that is *not speaking.* —NAOMI WOLF

Learning what's going on inside you can be difficult, but it's also invigorating, and the rewards are enormou

You can do anything if you only know what it is. And you're about to find out. —BARBARA SHER

NOTES